MICRODOSING FICTION

100 micro stories and prompts

by
Miguel S.

Copyright © 2024 Miguel S.

All rights reserved. This book or any portion thereof may not be reproduced or used in any manner whatsoever without the express written permission of the publisher except for the use of brief quotations in a book review.

ISBN: 978-80-11-05630-8 (Paperback)
ISBN: 978-80-11-05631-5 (Hardcover)

Any references to historical events, real people, or real places are used fictitiously. Names, characters, and places are products of the author's imagination.

Printed by Lulu Press Inc. Morrisville, North Carolina
First printing edition 2024.

Published by Michal Štěpán, Lipůvka 38 679 22
The Fiction Dealer
fictiondealer.substack.com

*To my wife, who gave me the inspiration
to write again.*

Introduction

You're holding my dream in your hands right now. I've been thinking about what to say in this introduction for a long time, and this seems appropriate. You're holding my dream and there's nothing to say but thank you.

The dream would only be half fulfilled and the introduction would mean nothing if you didn't read these lines.

When I found micro-fiction as a writing format, I fell in love. Writing micro-fiction daily helped me build a writing routine, and it provided tiny writing fixes that kept me sane through the endless editing of my novel.

Then I started Microdosing, an online project which was meant to provide inspiration to people and make them write everyday.

As the Microdosing Fiction concept gathered fans on Substack, the idea of turning the stories into a collection was born. But I wanted to make the collection unique, not just a bunch of stories in one book.

Then, one faithful evening about seven months ago, when I was brushing my teeth, it came to me. The whole Microdosing concept is based on giving people inspiration to write. Let's give the readers a space in the book to write so they can act on that inspiration. Every copy will be unique, and I can't wait to see yours filled with beautiful words.

Thank you again. I hope you enjoy it.

~Miguel

Microdosing Fiction

You'll find a hundred stories on the following pages, each accompanied by a prompt in a title, dosage, and a blank page.
Every single one of my stories stems from those prompts and it's there to inspire your own stories.
The dosage represents the maximum word count for the story, e.g. 50mg = 50 words. Writing is, fortunately, not the same as baking, so one extra word here and there doesn't hurt. If the story wants more, write more; nobody's counting.
The blank page is there for you. Write your micro-story or a poem. Draw something. Let your children destroy them. Make them your own.
Whatever you do with these pages, I would love to see it. Tag me on Instagram (@miguel.s.writer) or Substack (@miguels4).

Dealer's tips on Microdosing

If you have never written micro-fiction before, the goal is to tell a complete story, with a beginning, middle, and end, in a few words.
If I had to give you some tips on writing micros, they would be as follows:
- The story needs to be told with implications and hints; let the mind fill in the blanks,
- Forget descriptions; focus on emotions. Make the reader laugh, cry, or cringe in disgust,
- Don't listen to me; write what you love.

Use wisely, and most importantly, have fun.

Portrait

80mg

His wrinkled, spotted hands shook as he pressed the pencil to the paper. A couple of scribbles poured out of the tip. Fog covered his mind, yet the arm knew the lines. The sketching picked up a pace and features of a woman came to life on the page.

So familiar, yet so unknown. Tears flowed down his wrinkled face. He pressed a shaking fist to his temple.

Looking over dozens of her portraits, he asked: "Who are you?"

Friends

100mg

You met when you were six. Drinking soda, trading pokémons, having fun; best friends forever.

You're fifteen, arguing over girls, in love with the same, yet you shake hands—best friends.

You're in your twenties, and life slaps you around. A career or college, new friends and colleagues, but you party together—best friends forever.

The thirties come. Marriages and kids, no time for anything, the world spins rapidly. Months of not seeing each other, different lives—growing apart. Life went on, losses and wins, moving on and coming back.

Suddenly, you're sixty. Sipping beers, trading stories, having fun—best friends till the end.

Funeral

50mg

The coffin slowly settled into the fresh grave. I glanced from my picture to my crying family, their tears ripping the remainders of my soul apart.

"Are you ready?"

"Can't I at least say goodbye?" I asked.

The cloaked figure shook its head. "I'm sorry; we have to go."

Candle

100mg

The smell of candles and the crack of the leather belt don't go well together. For me, it was a match made in hell. I couldn't tell what my stepfather loved more – beating the shit out of me or his scented candles.

A six-pack of beer after a beatdown and a dozen scented candles burning. I used to snuff them out before bed, stopping the hungry flames from licking the curtains. Not anymore; I was done with him.

As the wheels of my suitcase rolled over the carpet, I spared him one last glance, and let it burn.

Cave

50mg

Dark shadows lurked in the mountain's depths. The orange blaze ripped the night's veil, keeping even the bravest heroes at bay.

Inside the cave, pocket dragons danced around the fire, chased their shadows, and occasionally spit a flamy burp into the night.

Accidental mirage ensured a peaceful life, free of humans.

Invitation

60mg

Edward walked Ella home like a true gentleman, even offering his coat as he barely felt the chilly air.

When they reached her house, he stopped at the door.

She looked at him with raised eyebrows.

"You didn't invite me."

"I invite you to my home, sir Edward," she laughed.

He smiled, revealing sharp fangs. "Rules are rules."

Pain

80mg

There's no pain similar to seeing your loved one wither. Emily and I were together for decades, our lives devoted to each other.

When the tremors began, our world imploded. I begged all deities I knew to take her pain away. "Let me take it on instead," I pleaded on my knees.

Emily came from the doctor's office today, joyfully skipping to me. "It's gone! The doctor said it's a miracle!"

"That's awesome, honey," I smiled, hiding my trembling hand.

Hearth

80mg

The wooden planks creaked under Dorian's feet, hands shaking. He looked around the empty inn. Instead of the usual music, there was a deafening silence. Only ghosts and shadows were left at the often full tables.

The ever-warm hearth was dead and cold, as were all the buildings in the village. Dorian's knuckles whitened and the parchment in his hand crumbled. An antidote, a solution to the plague, was in his grasp.

Alas, his journey was pointless, for he returned way too late.

Ghostwriter

100mg

Dozens of crumpled paper balls covered the exquisite carpet in my room at the Ritz. The frustration brewed as the inspiration eluded me.

After several hours of trying, I gave up and found refuge in the Hemingway bar.

One too many daiquiris later, my room welcomed me with the well known scratching of pen against paper.

My hazy mind couldn't fully process the lone pen dancing over my notes. I stumbled over, confusion rising as I watched the pen write:

There is nothing to writing. All you do is sit down at a typewriter and bleed. Good luck.

Dentist

100mg

Dr. Linda was polishing her dental tools in the moonlit clinic, prepared for her late-night patient.

The door creaked open, and a dark figure stood there unmoving.

Linda smiled. "Come on in."

With the invitation, the pale gentleman stepped inside, bloodied hand over his mouth.

"What happened?" Linda asked.

Instead of answering, the stranger revealed two long fangs, one of them split in half. "Can you help me?"

Linda gestured to the dental chair. "Fae teeth are tricky but I'll see what I can do." Helping centuries-old monsters wasn't the most moral work, but they paid well.

Glass

50mg

They say shards bring happiness — perhaps they do.

Since that corporate party.

Since the moment you knocked that glass out of my hand, staining your beautiful emerald dress with red wine.

Since we picked the shards out of the expensive carpet, laughing at each other.

Since then, I've been happy.

Sunlight

100mg

Demon hunters lived in shadows so others could enjoy the light. Axel knew that when he stepped on this lonely path twenty years ago.

Now wrinkled, covered in scars, with silver in his hair and beard, he took on one last demon. From dusk till dawn, the crypt shook with their battle.

Axel emerged victorious and sat on the stairs outside, pale as snow, the last drops of his blood escaped through his wounds. The warmth of the morning sunlight spread across his face, and peace filled his soul.

He closed his eyes, his breathing faltered. Rest at last.

Break

70mg

Drathok stepped into the hell's break room, leaving the eternal screams behind a closed door.

Calmness washed over him as he exhaled, decompressing from another shift of punishment. A cold beer and a Lakers game were so close. Two more torture sessions and he was done.

His watch vibrated and the break was over. With a deep breath, he opened the doors and let the screams embrace him.

Hourglass

50mg

Noah ran a bloodied thumb against the tattoo on his wrist – an hourglass almost empty.

He sighed, kneeling beside his wheezing opponent; this was always the worst part.

"I'm sorry," he said, tearing up, and drove the knife deeper.

The tattoo replenished itself with sand. Another life taken, another day gained.

Paper

100mg

A boy lived across the street from me. He loved paper planes. Any time a stranger went by, he folded one up and threw it into the street bearing a message. He brought a bit of sunshine into our neighborhood.

Despite his spreading baldness, despite his frail skin, despite the prison of his room. He still threw them, wishing people great days.

Last one I ever caught said only one word: Farewell. That day, the light stopped shining so bright.

It's been years now. I still stop by his gravestone every year and leave a tiny paper plane for him.

Veil

70mg

Wet mud swallowed Mark's knee and tendrils of mist clawed at his ankles. Moonlight glittered in the ring.

"Will you marry me?" he asked, madness glimmering in his dark-rimmed eyes; the cold stone block remained silent. "Please..." he begged, choking.

The veil between life and death ripped. A hand passed through, accepting the ring and Mark's soul with it, leaving his earthly body to rot at his lover's gravestone.

Chapter

60mg

A sense of pride filled Diana. Turning on a new page always takes a lot of courage, but she finally did it. Under the bright moon, with shoes drenched in mud, she made the change.

With her hands dirty and shovel sunk deep into the dirt, she exhaled, preparing for a new chapter of her life as a single lady.

Voicemail

100mg

The room was filled with nothing but silence. A bottle of whiskey on the table, a handwritten note next to it. A phone rang, piercing the unnatural muteness. The machine beeped, recording the voicemail.

"Hey dude, I know we haven't spoken in some time. I... look, I saw your video. Please just give me a call, okay?"

Another ring, another beep, and a trembling woman's voice spoke. "Hey Jeffrey, I wanted to make sure you're okay. I... please just call me back honey, yeah?"

Voicemails piled up until the machine's memory was full. The silence returned, disturbed only by a creaking rope.

Peace

60mg

I sat on a bench, all alone, breathing in purified air through my mask. The green lake in front of me reflected the weak fumes-covered sun.

No birds, no rustling leaves, no signs of life. Just silence. It was always silent. The world stood unmoving.

Who would've thought being the last human alive could be so peaceful?

Room

70mg

Dust settles. The room resets.

The haze slowly clears out of my withered brain. Exhausted and trapped, I shuffle back to my spot at the center. The familiar lines pop back into my mind. My wounds close up despite my wishes.

"Let's get this over with," I mutter as he enters the room, skipping over my evil monologue. We fight. I die. Next level.

Dust settles. The room resets...

Tower

90mg

The poster promised a tale as old as time — a princess in the tower, reward: a mountain of gold.

Jonathan didn't hesitate; the vision of gold clouding his brain and stuffing his ears. Oblivious to the lack of mountains and lakes he had to cross. Ignorant to the absence of the mighty dragon, he climbed the tower.

Clumsy Jonathan tumbled into the princess' room. The smell of rotten meat kicked him in the teeth. The gruesome growl of the hairy beast heralded his end.

Another victim of false advertisements.

Rot

60mg

Finn's steps echoed in the empty streets of London. Raspy coughs surrounded him, breaking the unnatural silence. The flowers and herbs in his beak did nothing to stop the stench of death.

The closer he got to his family home, the more his insides tightened. The moment he opened the door, the rotten air snuffed all hope.

Finn's knees buckled, tears filled his mask.

No need for a doctor anymore.

Imminence

100mg

Cheryl saw her on the day her mother died. The pale lady with ruby eyes grinned as Cheryl ran into the street. Her grin faded when Cheryl's mother saved her from the approaching bus.

Years later, she appeared again at the edge of the road, just seconds before Cheryl's boyfriend fell asleep behind the wheel. She stood by her hospital bed, frowning as doctors saved Cheryl's life.

Since then, she has been everywhere. In the passing cars, the windows, and the crowds. Closer every time, her grin widening.

Cheryl ran, but there was nobody to push her out of the way this time.

Wish

50mg

Lisa slid off of Riley. The night's air cooled their skin while they watched the falling stars.

"Wish something," Riley whispered.

"I wish tomorrow would never come," the wish escaped Lisa's lips, dissipating into the cosmos.

The stars obliged. Falling on Earth, they made it the last night in human history.

Old

100mg

With pale skin and frail bones, it made sense the hooligans would target me. To them, I was just a withered old man, skulking around the city's moonlit streets. My exquisite clothing likely made them assume I'd wear other riches on me.

Three "heroes" jumped me in the back alley. Their bats fell down on me repeatedly. I played along, asking for mercy with a trembling voice.

I'll admit I couldn't hold the ruse up for long. My laughter made them step back. My wounds mended, fangs grew in my gums. Fear scented the air.

What a feast it was that night.

Explosion

60mg

"MARY! MARY! MARY!" the crowd chanted.

Mary took a deep breath, her sweaty palms wrapped around the wooden handle of the bat. She took a swing.

Missed.

Children's laughter echoed in her ears. She focused, embracing the darkness of her blindfold.

With another swing, an explosion of candy erupted. The kids swarmed her, cheering.

Mary laughed. A perfect birthday.

Answers

80mg

Chasing answers was my life. The elusive spirits escaping me home after home. The questions were the same, always.

Who are you? Do I have your eyes? What do you do? Why did you leave me?

It took years before I finally found you. The hope of getting my answers got snuffed out as I watched you playing with your son, one big happy family. I got a new question instead.

Why did he get to grow up with you?

Family

50mg

We exchanged smiles and pleasantries around the table, hiding dramas under fake masks. Hunger for power and money shimmered in our eyes. The unfortunate events that brought us together were overshadowed by questions.

Who will get the will? Who was Daddy's favorite after all? Who drove in the dagger?

Statue

60mg

"Magnificent work," the Countess said, her hands running over the creases of the statue's face.

"So life-like," added the Count. "You've overdone yourself."

The sculptor bowed. "You are too kind," his voice sizzled like a snake pit.

Together, they moved to another exhibit in the collection. Followed by the statue's dead eyes, its screams for help silenced by the unmoving lips.

Haunted

60mg

The house grew dark, the kids were in bed, and the Jeffersons put on *The Haunting of Hill House*. I watched with them for a while; a pretty funny show.

When they finally went to sleep, I stretched my ghastly limbs. Another night shift of creaking floors, shattered mugs, and smashing doors began.

Sort of like the haunting of Jefferson house.

Drink

50mg

Jessie carefully stepped through the door, expecting yelling and fits of rage. It was the new normal.

She was waiting for him instead, dinner and drinks ready.

"Wow," he said.

"Negroni, your favorite!" she smiled.

Jessie, pleasantly surprised, drank. "It tastes like almonds..."

Her eyes glittered. "Yes. Yes, it does."

Necromancy

100mg

With dirt and grime stuck under Alexander's nails he watched the coffin. His insides were tight.

"We'll be together again. I promise."

He took out a black book. Insanity flashed in his eyes as the forbidden sentences escaped his lips.

The casket shook and the lid slid over. His lover rose up. Her skin pale, her lips purple, she looked almost intact—like the day he lost her.

"My love..." he said.

The corpse turned. She seemed to recognize him for a breath before sinking her teeth into his neck.

"We'll be together..." he gurgled, ignoring the pain and stench.

Tree

60mg

Faded M+K, a symbol of teenage naivety carved into the bark. Their promise of *forever* gone within the year of them kissing for the last time under that tree.

Years, graduations, jobs, and marriages later, only the letters and their memories remained.

Both were left wondering: What would've happened if I had returned to that tree? Just like we promised.

Mind

50mg

Pain and struggles tortured the artist's mind. Melancholy gnawed at his brain and guided his arm. Suffering fueled his brush, filling canvases with breathtaking beauty that captivated the masses.

The artist's life shifted, calming the storms inside him. His soul met happiness.

Suddenly, no color left the tip of his brush.

Cake

90mg

Freddy woke up in his cell with a wide smile. Today, he gets to see his wife, an early birthday present.

Hours passed, and his excitement faded. *She promised,* Freddy thought, a hole spreading in his chest. The guard's steps made Freddy push away the tears. The guard left a cake with a note in his cell, leaving Freddy alone.

The note said: *Sorry I couldn't make it.*

Freddy sighed. *At least she didn't forget me.* He took a bite, chipping his tooth.

A key peeked through the frosting.

Shovel

100mg

The shovel hit a tin can and excitement rippled through the group. Ten years after graduation, it was still there—a treasure of their youth buried in the school's yard.

Leslie brought the time capsule out and Jess eagerly snatched it from his hands. He loved that child-like curiosity about her.

Everybody looked over her shoulder, wanting to bathe in the memories and nostalgia. But Jess put the box aside, keeping only an envelope with her name. She snapped it open and a golden ring fell into her lap.

Leslie smiled. "I believed in us," he said, moving onto one knee.

Letter

50mg

The battle took months. We exchanged blows and waited to see what would happen. The waiting was the worst. I always over thought every move.

Today, I got another letter. Observing my opponent's fatal mistake, I couldn't contain my smile.

Hastily, I opened my pen and wrote: *Queen to H2. Checkmate.*

Party

60mg

The blood moon bathed the graveyard in crimson, coloring the swirling mist into burgundy. The god of Death, also known as Kevin, spread out his arms.

"Tonight. We party, my friends!"

The graves shook, dead awoken from their slumber. Kevin set the stage, turned the knob, and the music blasted until the G fell off the graveyard sign.

Quill

60mg

Soros lifted the Quill and the code of existence presented itself to him as a wave of power rippled through his flesh. He was a god now.

Insanity filled his eyes as he edited the core rules of reality. With just a couple of words, the world was his.

The Quill hummed happily, taking a day with every letter.

Stalker

70mg

Becca's pulse quickened, her hands rummaging in the purse. Cold sweat broke on her back as she dropped the keys.

His stare burned on the back of her neck. He stood across the street and watched, just like every night. He never approached; she just needed to get the keys quickly.

That night was different. She heard the footsteps echoing in the dimly lit street.

Gloom

70mg

"We called ourselves the gloomy boys. We've been those edgy guys, y'know? Listening to songs about depression and suicide, wearing all black. Joking about dark stuff; always joking-"

Joe's wife squeezed his hand, offering the impossible promise of comfort.

"They were just jokes, Mary... Stupid jokes!" sobs tremored through the last gloomy boy's body.

As the candle flames danced in unison on the graves of his friends, gone too young.

Cupcake

70mg

I stopped at my door, checking my phone one last time — 0 notifications. Another year passed and nobody cared.

With a sigh, I fumbled for the keys.

"Wait!" A cheery voice stopped me.

I turned and smiled at the lovely old lady from across the hall.

She motioned for me to stay and vanished into her apartment. She shuffled out again in a minute, smiling and holding a cupcake with a lit candle.

Awareness

60mg

Coming back from the toilet, the lights and loud music got me back into the party mood. The cute guy was still waiting on me.

I reached for my drink, noticing the plastic cover I put over it was gone. A charming, eager smile spread on his face.

I smiled back at him, ordering an Uber under the table.

Human

50mg

Karthol floated along the rings of Uranus, a beard of tentacles spinning around a human kebab. All sixteen of his eyes closed in disgust, fighting the urge to vomit over the Milky Way. He swallowed an entire city's worth.

Humans tasted awful, but they were the cheapest snack in the universe.

Shadow

100mg

My insides tightened as I approached the gloomy manor. Vines and moss slithered alongside the weathered walls. Our family home welcomed me with dust and stale air.

There he was, just a shadow of his former self, staring out of the window with glassy eyes. The state of the house reflected on his brain.

"Hi, Dad."

No reaction.

I knelt beside his chair. "Dad, they are all gone. The people that did this to you. We got them all."

It was too late for the curse to let go. Yet, his eyes glittered and he gave me a toothless smile.

Clock

100mg

Tim sat on the ground, swaying from side to side. Bloodshot eyes framed by dark circles pinned to the darkness. All clocks were stuck at 3:15 again, even the broken ones. Their chiming bounced in Tim's ears.

He squeezed his eyelids, trying to push the visions away, but they continued to haunt him. *One too many bottles. Shattered glass, blinking lights, the cars on fire. 3:15 stuck on his watch.*

"It was an accident..." he murmured into the silence, tears burning in his eyes. "Why can't you let me be..."

The clocks chimed louder, drowning him in his punishment.

Sword

50mg

The smoke stung in Lionel's eyes. "We are king's men. We are doing this for our kingdom. We are king's men. This is for our kingdom..." he kept repeating the words, fighting off the screams.

He raised his sword, bloodied to black, and entered another's family home in the village.

Harvest

50mg

The sky ripped open before giant reflective cubes landed in various places around the globe, annihilating forests and evaporating lakes in the process.

Each contained a tentacled monster known as the Outer Race.

All attempts at communication were futile. The Outer's came to harvest the livestock they planted there long ago.

Warrior

60mg

I glanced at the black bags hanging on my battlefield. "You are a warrior," my mother's voice echoed inside my skull.

I'm a warrior and I win.

A couple weeks later, I stroked my bald head, nerves settling in.

The doctor smiled at me. "We will keep a close eye on you. But for now. We've won."

Ghost

50mg

I shattered the mug I gave you, made my office floors creaking, and played the drums in the garage. I did so much to get your attention, but you just fled away frightened.

I'm sorry I scared you. I just wanted to say the final goodbye, my love.

Crew

60mg

There is nothing like the thrill of the hunting pack. Living on the edge with your brothers bonded by the blood of others.

For centuries, we have chased the weaklings like wild animals. Drunk on sweet human blood.

But they got too clever. We became desperate. Now I'm the last one standing here amidst empty coffins in the crypt.

Late

50mg

When Adriana cried for help, it came too late.

When they stopped the bullies, it was too late.

When she locked herself in a room, they came knocking too late.

When she felt the most alone, they were not there.

When they read the latter, it was too late. Again.

Flower

50mg

The machines beeped rhythmically. Joe was still sleeping as his body battled the unknown illness.

Mellisa put the flowers on his bedside table and planted a gentle kiss on his forehead as the nurse strolled by.

Fourth husband was dying like this, and pretending was not getting easier.

Curse

50mg

Clack.

Clack.

Clack.

The buttons slowly escaped the prison of his flannel shirt and the seams on his jeans followed soon after. Yet, he stuffed his face more and more. His body bloated, growing into grotesque sizes.

Many times, he tried to break the cycle and save himself. Yet, when the curse asked for another donut, he lost.

Deadline

50mg

A man stood on a bridge. His phone kept ringing. It was work again. They wanted to ask where he was and why he wasn't working.

The project needed to be done. Deadlines upon deadlines.

He took a breath and stepped into the void.

One final deadline to meet.

Soulmate

50mg

They stood next to each other at a concert. Each on their own. They sat in the same train, just a coach apart. They lived in the same building for a while and never met.

Their souls longed for the other; yet their paths never crossed, leaving them in the land of broken hearts.

Love

50mg

She peaked across the room, catching his glance. Both of them were reading the same book. She smiled at him, and he nodded at her, laughing.

They went through the same pages filled with romance and unlikely encounters, stealing quick side-eyes of one another.

It didn't take long until a conversation struck over a book full of love.

Kiss

100mg

Some nights are endless at the bars where nothing matters but the music and sweat. One can taste the passion in the air steaming from the people on the dance floor.

That's where Nick met her—or maybe she met him. He had no say in what would happen, but his fate was sealed when her eyes laid on him.

She floated through the crowded club, her steps otherworldly elegant. Time stopped when she came forward and leaned in for a kiss.

The world vanished as his soul escaped through his lips. Such is the power of a succubus.

Skull

100mg

The drunkard willed his vision to focus on the mighty black sword above the bar. "Y-You are the dragon slayer," he mumbled.

The barkeep chuckled. "You had one too many, my friend."

"No-no, I know you. You slayed the Kingdom's doom..."

A raised finger made him pause. The barkeep smiled, making sure nobody was listening. "I always wanted to have my own bar. Dragon slaying gets tiresome."

The drunk nodded as if he could understand, and then the realization kicked in. His eyes followed the cave-like surroundings, with two massive circular windows in the ceiling.

Suddenly, the name *Dragon's Skull Bar* made a lot of sense.

Chill

50mg

The darkness set in and my siblings' fangs sharpened. They were always seeking another artery, addicted to the thrill of the hunt.

Not my thing, though. I prefer to stop at the blood bank, put a straw in the fresh pack of AB negative, and chill at my crybt — Gen Z vampire style.

Paradise

70mg

Caroline sighed; the taste of freedom still fresh in her mouth, the last ripples of sea foam sizzling around her toes.

Her husband squeezed her hand, the same longing in his eyes. They wished the moment could last forever. But everything comes to an end.

With new memories still burning in their minds, they left paradise behind, returning to a life of spreadsheets and responsibilities.

Fire

50mg

The blaze hurt his eyes, yet he didn't look away. Tears rolled down his cheeks; the cause might've been the fire or the smoke.

Or maybe it was the memories burning away with her photos inside the flame.

Years of life turned into ashes with just one word – goodbye.

Game

60mg

They stared at each other, their hearts drumming. Only one of them could win this game.

A single drop of sweat fell from Tony's forehead. He felt the cold steel of the gun on his temple. The barrel spun.

Click.

Last empty chamber.

With a heart in his stomach, he met the eyes of his best friend and handed him the revolver.

Sunset

50mg

The sky turned crimson as the burning star sank beyond the horizon. The villagers cried and shivered with fear, praying to gods that didn't listen.

When the last rays of sunlight that kept them safe vanished, all went with it.

The monsters awoke and crimson spilled from the sky into the streets.

Addiction

50mg

One more spin.

Damn it! AGAIN!

One more spin.

Fuck! Again!

And so he spins—again and again—watching his car go, then his house, and his child's college fund.

With his last dollar, he stares at the machine; naive dreams of wealth are reflected in his eyes.

One. More. Spin.

Hide & Seek

50mg

"... Ninety-nine... One hundred! Ready or not, I'm coming!" Julian's voice echoed through the house before he left the room. His brother giggled under the bed just behind him. Sneaky little place.

"He will never find me!"

A raspy voice giggled next to him. "No. No, he won't."

Cage

70mg

Trapped in a cage, I was their plaything. My colors served as a decoration in their living room. My ability to mimic their voices became their entertainment. They laughed and jumped around like apes when "fuck" escaped my beak.

Their laughs got real silent when I continued, "Fuck-fuck me, Jeff. Your wife will never know!"

I cackled, watching them fight. Never a good idea to piss off a lying parrot.

Doll

50mg

I found a doll in the attic and brought it to the garage, preparing for the garden sale.

I found the doll on the couch in the living room. Even though I didn't bring it there. So, I threw it in the garbage.

The doll found me in the bedroom.

Diamond

80mg

"Diamond – that's the hardest material in the world, y'know?" the guy at the bar said. Diamond rolled her eyes, the same line used over and over.

"Never heard that one," she said and ignored his rumbling.

With his fragile ego hurt, he waited outside until her shift ended. As soon as she stepped out, he approached.

One bloody nose later, he found out it's also a name for the hardest girls.

Senior

100mg

Granny Bernadette always made the kids laugh. She spilled crazy tales about her faithful black cat and fables about her tiny hut above the village.

Today, she finished on a high note, her eyes covered in a milky haze, bright with excitement. She told the awestruck children about some lordling she had turned into a frog.

With bellies shaking with laughter, the kids went to sleep, and Bernadette's eyes turned from sparkly to gloomy.

"After that, they came. Forks and torches in hand, pyres ready..." she looked at me and winked, "but they never caught me."

Graveyard

90mg

Crazy ol' Charlie worked the graveyard's night shifts. He was a nice dude, but he often made up nonsense about moving dirt and hollow graves.

Nobody took him seriously. Charlie's love for whiskey was well known. But ol' Charlie stood his ground, pleading to the people that he wasn't crazy. Nobody listened.

One night, the hands poked out, and the dead raided the town. Crazy Ol' Charlie sat at the top of the graveyard's crypt, enjoyed his whiskey, and watched the graveyard's occupants expand their home to the town.

Mountain

70mg

A mix of snow and ice bit our faces. Frost-covered bones lined the path through the mountains.

A grim memento of the fools before us. We thought we would be different and make it in time.

But the cold giants, overlooking our foolish quest, decided to keep us. The avalanche came with a roar. Soon after that, there was little difference between a friend and food.

Lighthouse

100mg

The rumble of waves and salty air woke up Gregory; a pair of headlights and screeching tires were his last memories.

"G'evening, sir. 'ow was yer life?" an old fella in scruffy sailor's clothes asked.

"What-"

"Car crash, ey? That ain't pretty."

Gregory shook his head, looking at the colossal reflector. "Wait. Is this a lighthouse?"

The keeper laughed. "Where do ya think the light at the end of the tunnel comes from, eh? I'm here to guide lost souls an' ye look proper lost, matey!" Smiling, the lighthouse keeper grabbed Greg's shoulder and accompanied him on his final journey.

Home

60mg

They called it a home. A place full of love and safety. A sanctuary for the lost—such bullshit.

To me, it represented violence, split lips, and screaming. So much screaming.

In the very end, screams would make up my last memory of that place as I watched the flame tongues devour the whole house.

A matchbook heavy in my pocket.

Airport

100mg

Nerves trembled through my body; rivers of sweat drenching my shirt. *They will know. They will catch me. Act normal; just act normal!* The officers watched me with faces made of stone as I passed the gate.

Greenlight. *Now, just the bag.*

Holding my breath, I watched it go through the scanner. The officer glanced at me, then moved the bag closer.

His words washed all of the stress away. "Have a safe flight, sir."

I thanked him with a smile and got away. The beer can I had bought was still safely hidden in my clothes.

Screw you, overpriced airport bars.

Storm

100mg

Dark clouds veiled the sky, submerging the golf course in shadows. The horns blasted, accompanied by roaring thunder.

Every player must've heard that signal saying: *stop playing and get inside; the storm is coming.*

Phillip heard it, but he didn't care. One more hole and just a couple of shots held him from his best score ever. The thrill spoke against all senses, making him feel invincible.

He swung his seven iron, sending the ball right at the flag, hole-in-one in the making. But he never saw it fall in.

The sky split, and the lightning struck its own hole-in-one.

Consequences

60mg

Every action has its consequences, right? Bullshit. Why is he still free, then? Why can he walk the streets after what he did to me? No. I won't allow this anymore. I'll bring the 9mm of consequences myself!

Every action has its consequences, right? Apparently, making the world a better place lands you a concrete box with bars on the windows.

Academy

60mg

The application read: Welcome to a place for special children with unique talents and abilities! My heart beat a little faster. *Finally, a place where I belong.*

Finding out that their unique abilities meant excelling at math was a bummer. But I was already in and mind-controlling a school full of geniuses sounded like a lot of fun.

Compass

90mg

"I got this from you years ago and for ages, I thought it was just a circle with a needle, never showing anything," Jeff said, looking at the compass in his hand.

"One day, when it finally moved, it pointed to Hailey here," he choked on his next words, unable to continue.

Jeff's new wife sniffled beside him; he grabbed her hand and raised the little artifact towards the sky.

"Thank you for showing me the right direction, even if you can't be here today, Dad."

Scam

60mg

The vultures are circling around my treasure. I've sent a million emails by now, begging people to take my money.

Without a family, nobody can inherit my seventy million dollars, and I'm running out of time.

But nobody answers an email from the Nigerian Prince.

Drizzle

80mg

Raindrops beat against black umbrellas in a solemn rhythm. The casket sank into the fresh dirt. Tears streamed from under my sunglasses.

I knew it was for the best. We had to keep up the ruse and the illusion so you could finally be free and safe. Old life got buried, so a new one could start.

Through all of the pretending, the tears were real. Even though the casket was empty, I knew we'd never see each other again.

Punk

90mg

I stood in the bathroom, looking in the mirror at my fading hairline. The memories of my youth, filled with mohawks, graffiti, music, and drugs, were slowly fading away with it.

Now, locked in the life of cubicles, spreadsheets, nine-to-fives, and screaming jerk bosses. I hated everything about it.

Right there, something spurred in me, awaking the old times. I took out a sharpie and drew a massive penis on the mirror, with my boss's name right above it.

"Punk's not dead," escaped my lips before I handed in my two weeks' notice.

Embrace

80mg

Eleanor laid at the foot of the cliff, bones broken, body mangled, her neck twisted bizarrely. The ocean roared, overshadowing the wet cracks, as her body began to repair itself.

After a thousand tries, she didn't even feel the pain anymore. She didn't feel much of anything, living for millennia, yet walking the world as an empty shell of a being.

So alone in this world that not even Lady Death wanted to embrace her.

Space

50mg

So many of our ships burned in the stratosphere. Billions spent and years of our lives sacrificed just to finally pierce the sky's veil, and be the first living being in space.

When our final rocket finally reached the stars, we realized. We're not the first. Not by a mile.

Grime

50mg

Black fingers, grime under my nails, life spent around wrenches and roaring engines. That was a mechanic's life—a life that siphoned every ounce of joy from me.

It took me years to finally pursue my passion. My fingers are still black but now stained with ink and dreams.

Dragon

70mg

All it took was a single drop to awaken the dragon in him. One sip of brown liquid and the monster broke out of its cage.

The peaceful father was replaced by a tyrant with a leather belt, leaving bruises on the body and soul of his family.

Tyranny can't last forever. In the end, all it took was a single drop to put the dragon to sleep — forever.

Superstition

100mg

On the morning of Friday the 13th, I woke up shivering. Visions of my old human in danger seared fresh under my eyelids. *She can't go to the market today,* I thought to myself.

A door slammed shut. She was already on her way. Without hesitation, I rolled in the fireplace, the soot sticking to my fur, and then, I ran out after her.

I crossed her path once, twice, three times, until she turned to go back home. I got there first, breaking a mirror and spilling salt.

Maybe I was just as superstitious as she was, but it kept her safe.

Box

80mg

Boxes changed Johnny's life. First came the box of wine they found under his table at work. Followed by the box he took with him, along with the termination of his contract.

Soon after, he got a box of his belongings, and the doors of his own home shut forever behind him.

Then, there was that one cardboard box serving as an excuse for a shelter.

And finally, when the end came, he didn't get a box to rest in.

Waiting

80mg

The waitress came to ask me if I wanted to order. Again. The pity in her beautiful blue eyes was so palpable I had to look away. "She is not coming, is she?" I asked, desperation in my voice.

"I don't know," she smiled and handed me the menu. A slip of paper fell out, *My shift ends in an hour.*

Years later, a piece of paper slipped under my door, *See you at the altar in an hour.*

Facade

100mg

Cuddled together, the children strayed through the forest. Their tender bodies shivered with hunger. A ball of weak light in the distance, fighting against the setting darkness; their only hope.

Excited smiles spread on their faces, sharp and wide, as they reached the light, and an old lady in her hut welcomed them.

The granny smiled at them, her door stood always open, and she was always ready to help.

She rushed them inside, bolting the door shut, before lighting the fire under an oversized cauldron.

The children giggled, fangs growing in their gums. The facade worked. It was a great feast that night.

Twins

50mg

My face stared back at me from the casket, flooding my mind with an avalanche of memories.

Everything since birth has been lived by two souls and when one got snuffed out, the other went, too.

Now, life seems empty and cold; any feeling just reminds me that I'm already dead.

Bottle

80mg

The dust settled, the stones stopped falling, and the explosions faded a couple of days ago. Yet, Marquis and Ellie still sat hurled in their broken home, waiting.

Ellie coughed. "I'm thirsty, daddy," she said, her voice dry and raspy.

Marquis nodded with a smile, trying to hide the tears from his daughter. He handed her their bottle, leaving her those last precious drops of water they had; knowing well that help is not coming.

Writer

50mg

"Hey, wanna go for a beer?"

"Sorry, I have to write."

"Wanna go golfing?"

"Sorry, I have to write."

"Babe, wanna watch a movie?"

"Sorry, I have to write."

And so he writes, burying himself in the trenches made of ink and paper, writing off people around him one by one.

Bureaucracy

100mg

Chris woke up in a room made of light, with only a desk and a grumpy-looking lady smoking a cigarette.

"Hello?" he asked, the confusion rising.

Instead of an answer, she just smashed a pile of papers on the desk. "Fill in the 1004, 290-new_soul form and then the form 4NG3-L. Also, show me your soul ID and the afterlife entrance form signed and stamped."

Chris blinked. "I'm sorry, I don't have any of that."

"Then I can't help you. NEXT!" the lady yelled and hit the red button on her desk, sending Chris back into the limbo of the souls.

Snack

50mg

As the centuries-old trees wrapped their arms around them, a blanket of silence engulfed their world. A sense of adventure and excitement filled their naive young souls.

They joked and giggled, unaware of the dangers in the woods. Unaware of the eyes following them.

Unaware that teenagers are his favorite snack.

Drowsy

90mg

My eyes were glued shut when I woke up. The house was unnaturally quiet for a Sunday. Kids were usually running around at this point.

Well, I didn't mind the peace. I made myself a cup of coffee and kept my pajamas on – lazy Sunday vibes.

I switched on the TV. A morning segment had just begun and I almost drowned in my coffee. The drowsiness slipped away instantly.

"We wish you a great start of the week on this fine Monday," the TV host said.

Punishment

60mg

You crossed a line, Joe-boy! You know what we do with stealing rats!

The voice of his boss rang in his mind as the concrete around his ankles hardened. They continued to bounce around even as the depths ate him whole.

He didn't expect to live his immortal years at the bottom of the sea.

Tears

70mg

"I cheated."

"I don't love you anymore."

"I never really did."

With every lie, my heart shattered. Each word cut deep wounds into her soul. I wish it could've gone differently.

As her anger grew, tears were soon replaced by screams and she kicked me out of the house.

It was for the best. Now she'd remember me as an asshole rather than a soulmate gone too soon.

Voodoo

100mg

Being a witch could hardly pay the bills. So, working a corporate job – which I hated dearly – was the only way to feed me and my feline friends. The meetings especially were bringing me excruciating amounts of pain.

One day, I brought the pain back by accident.

As my boss mumbled something about revenue, he suddenly cried in shock. A sharp claw-like scar appeared on his cheek, then another on his suit. In a breath, the whole meeting room was filled with screaming people.

The realization hit me like a ton of bricks; I left the basement open. And forgot to hide the dolls.

Tent

100mg

Being in the woods is a magical but fearsome experience, especially when it's dark, and the nearest civilization is miles away. The forest moves, whispering the secrets buried among the tall trees.

When the footsteps approach, the shivers run down your back in the tent. The rational mind kicks in first—probably just a deer.

Then something rummages through your stuff. Again, the mind thinks of animals—a raccoon at best, a bear at worst.

But when the zipper of your tent begins to open, you start to realize—animals can't open stuff. And they don't have long fingers with bloodied claws.

Disguise

100mg

Police did their best to keep the onlookers away from the house cordoned off with yellow tape. The nosy neighbors were resilient, though, looking for a chance to overhear the forensics or just peek through the window.

A man in a trench coat entered the crowd. "What happened here?" the stranger asked.

"Total massacre inside, gangs doing gang shit. All they found was a severed finger and a barrel full of acid," one of the neighbors whispered.

The stranger nodded and slightly adjusted his mustache with a four-fingered hand. "Poor guy," he said, smiling.

"Poor guy indeed."

Acknowledgments

No amount of thank yous will ever really show how thankful I am for writing these lines.
I have to start with a huge thank you to my wife Karolína for having the patience with me and my scribbling, for always having my back, and for putting the pen back into my hand when I don't feel like writing.
Thanks to my best writing friends Romana and Lenka who were there for me not only with all of my writing troubles but also helped me with proofreading the collection.
A massive thank you to the paid subscribers of the Fiction Dealer. Your support fueled a lot of the work on this book. So thank you, Gloria, Jack, Bob, Lia, and Colin, your support goes a long way. Special thanks to Nick for being the biggest donor of coffee.
I also need to thank the microdosing community

of Substack. Especially those who were there when the Fiction Dealer opened his lab and began cooking these microdoses of fiction. All of the support I received when the project started was the driving force that kept me going. So thank you, Patricia, Carolyn, Reginald, Viam, Mallory, Honeygloom, Barrie/Mr. Fables, Rolando, Saumya, Richard, Chris, Ej Trask L.L. Ford and Dustin.

I would love to name all of the microdosing regulars but I would soon run out of space. If you ever contributed to my online microdosing, thank you.

Subscribe to the Fiction Dealer for a daily dose of fiction!

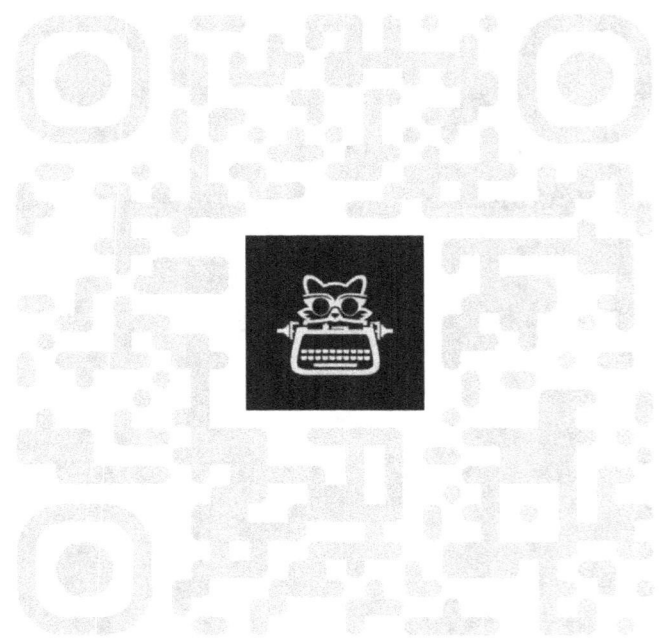

www.ingramcontent.com/pod-product-compliance
Lightning Source LLC
Chambersburg PA
CBHW071207240526
45470CB00018B/1534